Yacoub Aljaffery

Extended Relationships in Arab and American Cultures

GRIN Publishing

Bibliographic information published by the German National Library:

The German National Library lists this publication in the National Bibliography; detailed bibliographic data are available on the Internet at http://dnb.dnb.de .

Imprint:

Copyright © 2010 GRIN Verlag GmbH
Print and binding: Books on Demand GmbH, Norderstedt Germany
ISBN: 978-3-656-89391-2

This book at GRIN:

http://www.grin.com/en/e-book/289083/extended-relationships-in-arab-and-american-cultures

GRIN - Your knowledge has value

Since its foundation in 1998, GRIN has specialized in publishing academic texts by students, college teachers and other academics as e-book and printed book. The website www.grin.com is an ideal platform for presenting term papers, final papers, scientific essays, dissertations and specialist books.

Yacoub Aljaffery

Extended Relationships in Arab and American Cultures

Relationships are a part of everyday life. Regardless of culture or ethnicity, relationships between people can be seen across the globe. It is a defining characteristic of the human race. However, there are specifics on how these relationships are formed and to what extent. There are unspoken rules that govern everything from how people greet each other to the roles that they play in society. Although the Arab people share the same culture, there are differences within the culture from country to country. In this paper, we will concentrate on similar Arab practices in neighbor relationships and student and teacher relationships in the Gulf region and in northern Africa, specifically Sudan. These customs will then be compared to the parallel relationships found in America.

Relationships among neighbors:

Relationships in the Arab world are very intimate. People tend to help each other in many ways. Neighbors help each other. They tend to share their happiness and sadness in all occasions. Arabs in general try to look at society as a whole and not as a part. There are certain times of a day neighbors visit each other to ask about how they are doing and if they are in need of anything. In the Arab world, there are customs that are generally similar but with a few minor differences. This can be seen in how neighbors greet each other, visits among neighbors, and the welcome new neighbors give each other.

Because of the hot climate in the Arab countries, especially in the summer, life becomes active in the cool times of the day. In the Gulf region, people get up with the rooster's sounds. After breakfast, neighbors start to visit each other and see how they are doing. If one person is sick and cannot go to the hospital, one of the neighbors most likely takes care of that. If a person is in need of food and cannot afford to buy it, one of the neighbors or more than one volunteer to take care of the crisis. Usually the head of the family, whether it is the father or the older brother, goes to the next door neighbor. They greet each other by shaking hands and kissing the cheeks three times if it is between two people of the same gender. The cheek-kissing style is different from one country to another. In Iraq, for example, they give three kisses from one side to another and sometimes end it with touching each other's shoulders. However, in Saudi Arabia the kissing style is a little bit different. They start with one cheek and then kiss the other cheek three times in a row. They sometimes end it with touching each other's noses. Depending on the country and the religion people practice, greeting between men and women can vary. In some rural areas in Iraq, women do not cheek kiss men or even shake hands unless the man is part of the family. In cities like Basrah or in the capital, Baghdad, women shake men's hands or even cheek kiss them because of the many religions practiced in Iraq. In strict Muslim countries like Saudi Arabia, a woman shaking a man's hand is very rare and even impossible.

Sudan is similar to the Gulf region. People rise later in the day and tend to stay up late into the night. The method of greeting is alike, though. Cassie, an American who went to Sudan to work with education for 4 ½ months, describes one of her experiences with a neighbor:

> When I'd be walking home from a day of teaching, sometimes I'd see my university-aged female neighbor on the street. We'd stop in the street and greet each other. A Sudanese greeting among females consists of grasping hands or shoulders, saying "*Salaam aleekum*" and kissing the person's right cheek, then their left, then their right. Then the two continue to clasp hands during the inquiries into each other's well-being and families. After this, we would spend time conversing about other matters before parting ways.

In Arab greetings, one thing to note is the time people take for each other. The greeting is extensive and this shows that the relationship is valued. They spend at least a few minutes asking about each other's families and health in order to show that they care. A great importance is placed on these relationships, more so than the tasks you have to accomplish. To simply wave in passing would be rude.

In America, waving is the norm in greeting. A typical interaction between neighbors could be as simple as a smile and a wave. Often, when passing each other they will acknowledge each other's existence and keep going. If they know the person on a more personal level, they might stop and ask how they're doing. Typically, though, the lifestyle of an American is hectic and this does not leave room for extensive greetings. In addition, many Americans would feel that lengthy questioning about each other's families and lives would be crossing a boundary of privacy.

One cross-cultural example of the misunderstanding that can come from greetings is when I went to visit Iraq after living in the US since 1996:

> I got used to the short American greeting and waving. I used the same
> style in Iraq but people did not like it. People thought I was arrogant,
> they thought I was not humble and that I did not want to take two
> minutes to talk to them and ask about how they are doing.

The trends seen through these greeting styles is that the Arab culture puts more emphasis on people and relationships while the American culture puts emphasis on tasks and getting things done. There is also a difference in how neighbors visit each other.

Arab neighbors tend to share life difficulties and celebrations. They support each other during the good and the bad times. In a typical visit, neighbors stop by each other's houses. They sit down, talk about life, and have some coffee or tea to drink. All of the neighbors know each other and visit each other in times of illness, funerals, weddings and other life events. In an interview about neighbor relationships, one Saudi female said, "The neighbors in Saudi Arabia are very kind. They always help each other, ask about each other. They are beside you in every situation."

In a visit between neighbors, there are a few customs to be observed. In Iraq, for example, it is custom to send visitors away with fruit as a parting gift. In Sudan, at the end of a visit, tea is served to hydrate and as a sign that the visit is coming to a close. The length of visits should also be noted. In Iraq, a daily visit among neighbors normally takes about half an hour. However, if the neighbors haven't seen each other for a week then they would spend the afternoon together and share a meal together. In Sudan, long visits are also usual. A visit tends to take a couple of hours and is focused on conversation. In Arab neighborhoods, the conversation can center on neighborhood news.

Apart from normal gatherings, neighbors also gather in instances of illness, condolence and celebrations. During her time in Sudan, Cassie had the following experience:

> When our neighbor's *haboa*'s (grandmother's) sister died, the
> mourning was a very elaborate affair and many people came to visit
> the family and mourn with them. As neighbors, all of us American

3

girls paid respects by visiting the family and spending time offering
our condolences. It was expected that we would visit within the first
24 hours if possible to show our support and care. The mourning
period went on for about a week, during which the whole
neighborhood stopped by to visit the family.

Another example of the relationship between neighbors would be the generosity
among neighbors. They share everything including their food. Women tend to be
more generous than men. They will sell their jewelry or valuable belongings if there
is no other option in order to help their neighbor during a crisis.

In American culture it seems to be more of an inconvenience when people just
drop in to say hello. They prefer things to be scheduled. If they do stop over, the
visits tend to be brief. Conversations are usually light and people try to not pry.
Unless a person brings an issue to the table, the neighbors will refrain from talking
about heavy situations.

Gatherings among neighbors in an American context are centered on activities.
These could include graduation parties, bonfires, BBQ's, block parties and other
celebrations. Kate, an American student, had the following experience:

When I was younger, my mother and the neighborhood mothers (a
group of about 10) would all get together on Thursday mornings. They
would bring snacks and discuss the current novel they were reading or
hold a Bible study. Afterwards, they would spend time socializing and
catch up on what was going on in each other's lives without being
intrusive.

Upon reflecting on American customs, it is seen that Americans enjoy spending time
with other people, including their neighbors, but the occurrences are planned
occurrences and the relationships are more fragmented. They have a boundary of
certain times and places.

In Arab cultures, people tend to stay in the same neighborhood for a long
period of time, if not for the rest of their lives. One Sudanese woman reported that
she lived in her neighborhood for 32 years. Two Saudi students who attend Saint
Cloud State University lived in their neighborhoods for 8 and 14 years, respectively.
In Iraq, my family lived in the same neighborhood that their ancestors grew up in. All
of the interviewees stated they knew every family in their neighborhood. When asked
about how well they knew their neighbors, the Sudanese woman said she knew 3 of

4

the 10 neighbors very closely and the rest pretty well. The Saudi female commented that she knew her neighbors quite well as they had visited each other weekly and discussed current life events. The Saudi male said that he knew all of the neighbors' names and that they gathered together at different times. I, personally, knew my neighbors back home very well who lived in a close vicinity to the point that he didn't knock on the door before entering into the house. This is significant because the culture requires a person to knock on the door to allow women time to cover themselves. However, I was viewed as part of the family.

In the case where a new family moves into the neighborhood, they are welcomed in a very special way. Neighbors cook food for the newcomers for several days until they are settled in. In Iraq for example, the new resident receives meals for seven days. Each family cooks one or two meals a day until the new resident gets settled and accommodates to the new life. Neighbors usually visit the new family every day and sometimes they visit more than once during the day to make sure the newcomers are not feeling left out or in need of anything. A Saint Cloud State student from Saudi Arabia said they offer as much as they can to the new neighbor for three days and that they "offer them transportation, food and a tour through the new neighborhood if it's necessary". Other Saudi Arabian students said they greet the new neighbors and hold a weekly dinner in which the whole neighborhood attends. This provision of meals is also seen in Sudan. Arabs claim that the main purpose in doing this is so the new resident feels at home, loved and like they are not a stranger. This cultural practice is also seen in Islam. In one Hadeeth, the prophet Mohammad said, "Your neighbors, then your neighbors, then your neighbors, then your home." The prophet Mohammad emphasizes the neighbors three times, and then says your home. In some of the other Hadeeths, it narrates that Mohammad used to check if his neighbors had food to eat before he ate anything. The Sudanese interviewee made the following comment, "In Arab culture and Islamic instructions especially, one should welcome his new neighbor and receive them generously."

People in America have different experiences in their neighborhoods. The Americans that were interviewed lived in their neighborhoods for various lengths of time. For example, one 18-year-old informant has lived in her current house for 15 years. Others reported living in their neighborhoods for 18 years, 15 years, and 9 years. While the informants did not know their entire neighborhood, they did know a significant number of neighbors ranging from 15 neighbors to 6. The extent of their relationships was different for each person. One interviewee from a small town knew most of the neighborhood very well as many neighbors were family. Another responded that she knew 3 families well. In the case of the third respondent, she stated that her family knew 3 other families very well and kept in contact with them but that 5 or 6 were not as close.

Compared to Arab countries, there is a difference between how new neighbors are received in American society. None of the survey responders noted any practices for welcoming. Two had been welcomed themselves when they originally moved into their neighborhoods by neighbors who assisted with building the deck and by neighborhood children coming over to play. However, there are no set American customs with welcoming neighbors. This was a foreign concept to me, whose family had the following experience:

> When I first moved into the New Brighton neighborhood, our
> neighbors didn't come and greet us for several days. It was a big shock
> for us not to be welcomed the way that we experienced at home. Until
> today, we haven't had any strong relationships with our neighbors. In
> fact, we approached them on so many occasions and we brought
> presents for them during Christmas to break the ice and build a good
> neighbor relationship. But sadly, they didn't respond back

This type of transition into a new neighborhood can be a shock to people who come from different countries.

In both cultures, American and Arab cultures, neighbor relationships are valued but in different ways and are expressed differently. In the Arab culture, a person's everyday existence is intertwined with those around him. A neighbor is not just someone who lives in the same area; they are more like a family. In America, the neighbor relationship is viewed more distantly. There are occasions during which neighbors spend time together, but Americans have more of a 'take it or leave it' attitude. Their busy lifestyles promote the value of being independent from those around them even though they enjoy gathering together for different activities. For an Arabic person moving to the United States, he or she will find difficulties accommodating to this new lifestyle and view of neighbors.

6

Relationships among students/teachers:

In addition to discussing the relationships between neighbors in Arab culture and American culture, one must note another important relationship: the relationship between students and teachers. In both cultures, education plays a role in a person's life as they grow towards becoming adults. Due to this, the interactions between teachers and students play an important part in the lives of learners. In the two distinct cultures there are also two distinct approaches to the student/teacher relationship. As in any comparison, there are similarities and differences in the role of teachers as well as the amount and to what extent teachers and students interact outside of the classroom. One such distinction is that in the Arab world, Islam has an influence on how teachers are viewed.

The prophet Mohammad said in one of his Hadeeths: "Stand up for your teacher, your teacher has almost become a messenger." Also, Mohammad is called "the teacher", and the Muslims believe that he is a gift of Allah. Because of these hadeeths, people have profound respect for teachers. Arabs also believe that teaching is the master of other jobs. They believe that without teachers, the world would not have doctors, engineers or any other occupation. In general, families and students respect teachers. They consider them not only people that teach materials and books but teachers are considered people who raise a new generation. The behavior of the students when they grow is reflected on the teacher's behaviors and the way of teaching. One Sudanese woman describes the expectations of a teacher in Arabic culture in the following way: 'Teachers are expected to be nurturing as well as understanding of the needs of different developmental stages, for example, childhood and adolescence.' Teachers have a bigger role in a school than just teaching. In Iraq, they are responsible for the cleanliness of the students. Teachers take about five minutes every morning to check the student's hair, nails, teeth and clothes. There is also a certain rule for hair lengths in schools. Teachers can prevent students from coming back to school if he or she has long hair or dirty nails. Also, a teacher can cut the student's hair if it is required. In addition to how a teacher is viewed in general, the students have specific behaviors towards teachers.

Most of the students in Arab countries keep their respect for their teachers even if the student graduates from college. In Iraq, for example, they keep calling them "Master" and show respect through nonverbal communication. The Sudanese

7

woman also comments on the expectations of a student towards a teacher: 'Students are expected to be polite, assiduous in studying, and to obey and respect their teacher.'

> When I went to Iraq this past summer, my middle school math teacher came to visit me. When I saw him I talked to him differently than other people who were there in the room. I acted like he was still my teacher and put a border line in our conversation. He was not just a normal person. He was the key to get me to where I am at in my education.

There are certain behaviors that students practice to show their respect for their teachers. One of the ways that younger students show respect in Iraq is through greetings. At the start of the class, the students greet the teacher with a group slogan. When the teacher enters the room, all of the students get up and say their daily slogan that is usually prepared by the class "supervisor". The class supervisor is a student that is chosen by the teacher to take over the class if he/she is gone or during the five minutes break between classes. The following is one of my memorable experiences when I was in elementary school in Iraq:

> I was always chosen to be the class supervisor from first to fourth grade. I had to come up with greetings every day to have students recite when the teacher came into class. One of the greetings that stick in my head is when the teacher comes I stand by the board and shout 'Stand up'. The students get up and say, 'We show complete obedience,' then I say, 'Sit down,' and the students say, 'Miss Nahawand is the light of the class,' then usually the teacher gives feedback to students and thanks them in return

The role of the teacher in American culture is primarily as an educator. Compared to other countries, the role of the teacher is limited. There are many stipulations a teacher has to follow and barriers they have to be aware of. In this context, a teacher has to be careful of not crossing boundaries. However, a teacher can still act in the role of a mentor, a role model to students who don't have positive adult figures in their lives, a mandated reporter and a listener. This may be particularly important in schools that are located in places like the inner city. In the words of Kate:

> A teacher is viewed as somebody that will help you become academically intelligent. They will be there if need be. There are

8

many expectations we have for teachers in America. Some are to be understanding, compassionate, respectful, knowledgeable and organized. Teachers are a good resource for issues students are dealing with outside of the classroom, but are not meant to build close relationships out of the classroom with the students. This is due to the rules and regulations educational system in the United States.

While restricted, the role of the teacher is still an important one in the lives of students although they may be valued differently than in Arab countries. The roles of teachers vary from culture to culture, as does the way a student shows respect towards a teacher.

Respect is shown in an assortment of ways in American schools. When children are younger in American schools they are more attached and like attention from their teacher. They greet the teachers in the morning and may be excited to share their daily happenings with their teachers. In order to show respect and affection towards their teachers, young students may give gifts to them around holidays. Another way the child shows respect is by obeying classroom rules. As American students move through school, they show respect by being on time to classes, actively participating in classes and being quiet when necessary. A teacher is not automatically given respect from students. Students often challenge teachers and respect is usually given if it is earned. The teachers in America are seen as more personable and humble than teachers in Arab culture. The role of a teacher can be reflected in the relationships of students and teachers in each culture.

The relationship between students and teachers in the Arab world is carried over outside of the classroom. In the classroom, deference is shown to the teacher. The relationship between the two inside of a classroom centers on academic things. A student may approach a teacher to talk about a subject or a problem the student may not have understood. The strictness seen in teachers only occurs while in the school but when students meet with their teachers outside of school, the relationship becomes more like a family while still keeping the same high level of respect for the teacher. As one female student from Saudi Arabia says, "If the teacher is strict we have to listen to her and we should not talk to her about any other subject. But if the teacher is friendly and kind we can talk to her and let her be just like our sister or mother." It is important to note that students and teachers do have interactions outside of the classroom. This often takes the form of visits. In rural Iraq, it is common for a

9

teacher to visit the student and the student's family in their home and vice versa. Relationships can be closer in rural areas between teachers and students.

> When we were released from school, we didn't have buses to take us home. My house was far from school. My teacher, who used a horse as transportation, used to take me to my house.

Another example of the relationships between students and teachers outside of the classroom is given by the Saudi female student. When asked to describe what activities she and other students would do with her teacher, the student said, "We would have dinner, go to malls together or visit her in her home." In Sudan, the interactions vary a bit. The Sudanese female who responded to the questions given said that there was not as much close interaction between students and teachers in public schools due to crowded classrooms and the cost of transportation. She mentioned that in private schools, there is more contact between the teacher and student as well as the student's family and that the family might invite a teacher to visit their home. In Cassie's experience in Sudan, a teacher being invited to visit the student's home was not uncommon. This extended view of relationships between the teachers and students is not seen in America.

It is very abnormal for an American student to see their teachers in a setting other than in the classroom or school activities. It is certainly crossing the boundaries if a student and a teacher were to spend time together outside of the classroom. Although teachers are a good resource for students to talk to, students often prefer to speak with their peers. Teachers are more conservative in their relationships with students due to the consequences that could potentially occur. Things such as lawsuits and misconduct on the part of the teacher have to be kept in mind. The teacher is aware that every attempt should be made to protect themselves and their students so that these situations will not occur. Due to this, the relationship between a student and a teacher is strictly professional and academic and is not carried outside of the school setting. Parent-teacher relationships are formal and provide updates that concern the student. Face-to-face contact usually only occurs during scheduled parent-teacher conferences or if concerns need to be addressed. Other interactions between the family of a student and the teacher are at school-related activities such as field trips, PTA meetings, fundraising events and the like.

Implications for the ELL classroom:

ELL teachers carry a big responsibility in and outside their classroom. Understanding and interpreting an English language learner's culture is a very important part of an ELL teacher's role. It might seem easy to learn someone's culture, but it is hard in practice and to apply in reality. The task that ELL teachers carry is not only teaching the ELL students English, but also helping them outside of the class to accommodate to the new school environment. Misinterpretations can possibly occur on both sides. Whenever a mainstream staff member thinks an ELL youngster's behavior seems bizarre, rude or in some way unexpected, it is most likely a sign of cultural misunderstanding. And it is the ELL professional who is called upon to unlock the cultural puzzle.

There are many things ELL teachers should consider when their class includes students from an Arab background. Besides knowing religious celebrations and holidays, ELL teachers should be aware of the student's family and community relationships. How an Arab student is treated in his community and among his neighbors can completely influence his/her behavior inside the class. In addition to the family and neighbor relationships, knowing about an Arab student's life in school in their home country can unlock many issues that might seem ambiguous between student and teacher. ELL teachers should also realize how Islam has a considerable effect on Arab students inside the classroom and their behavior towards their teacher.

Upon arriving in the United States, an Arab student may go into shock when he sees how an American classroom is run. It is a vastly different experience from how classes are run in the Middle East. One such remembrance of this shock comes from an experience I had:

When I first moved to the U.S., I went to high school in San Diego. The class seemed to be chaotic, not organized and not controlled by the teacher. Students talked to each other in the class, sat cross-legged and did not really show any respect to the teacher. At the same time, I felt so isolated and that I didn't have my teacher listen to me at all. I thought I couldn't make it and I couldn't do school in America. That's the reason I dropped out of school here and went to Syria to finish high school.

In light of the experiences of Arab students, it is important to bridge the gap between cultures. One way an ELL teacher can do this is by being structured in their classroom as well as strict in homework assignments and making sure the students are staying on task and following the rules. This helps the Arab students to respect the teacher. While keeping this in mind, it is also important to be approachable. An ELL teacher should be kind, compassionate and a good listener to these students. Their backgrounds and life situations are varied and adjusting to a new country is a difficult thing. Many of these students and their families feel cut off from the types of relationships that were integral to their every-day lives back home.

One avenue of reaching out to these students is through their families. Teachers need to approach students through the families and have open communication with them. Usually students do not show their emotions if they are going through a hard time, but knowing the family can say a lot about the students. Since a teacher in the United States has to be cautious with the laws and ethics concerning student/teacher relationships, it may not be advisable to visit the student's home. Instead, a teacher can hold a family night for the students in their class at the school. This could be done once a month to help build relationships with the family and the student.

Another thing an ELL teacher can do to help the family's transition into American culture is to make them aware of ways they can connect with the community. This could be in the form of sending a weekly newsletter in both English and Arabic home to the family. The newsletter could detail community events, volunteer opportunities, local community education classes and any other services to help them build relationships with those around them. A teacher could also invite the parents to chaperone field trips or be more involved with activities in the school. This would give the parents a chance to connect with other parents in the school community. A third way to encourage community bonding is by attending various events in the Arab community, such as an Eid celebration.

In the classroom, an ELL teacher can motivate students to build a classroom community by teaching about various cultures. One week the class could focus on one culture and the next week, it could focus on a different culture. This way, students from a myriad of cultures can be inspired to grow in their knowledge and respect of their peers' cultures. In a practical application, the teacher could include reading materials such as an article or poem about Ramadan.

Conclusion:

A person's culture can take many shapes and forms. It influences many aspects of their lives, such as how they behave towards others. In addition to other practices, relationships also have cultural distinctions. As seen in the discussion, relationships between neighbors and also students and teachers are quite different in Arab and American cultures. Through growing in one's knowledge about the centrality of these relationships in Arab culture, an ELL teacher can be more effective in connecting with the student. They can also help ELL students to conquer homesickness and culture shock. In turn, this sensitivity towards the student and the Arab culture can be vital to the student's success. My ELL teacher was "the key to get me to where I am at in my education."